WELCOME TO THE WORLD OF

Moose

Diane Swanson

Whitecap Books

Vancouver / Toronto

Edited by Elizabeth McLean
Cover design by Steve Penner
Cover photograph by Thomas Kitchin/First Light
Interior design by Margaret Ng
Typeset by Susan Greenshields
Photo credits: D. Lehman/First Light iv; Chris Harris/First Light 2, 26;
Craig Brandt 4; Aubrey Lang 6; Wayne Lynch 8, 10; Victoria Hurst/First Light 12;
Thomas Kitchin/First Light 14, 18, 20; Tim Christie 16, 22, 24

Printed and bound in Canada

Canadian Cataloguing in Publication Data

Swanson, Diane, 1944–
    Welcome to the world of moose

    Includes index.
    ISBN 1-55110-854-2

    1. Moose—Juvenile literature. I. Title.
QL737.U55S92 1999   j599.65'7   C98-911024-9

For more information on
this series and other
Whitecap Books titles,
visit our web site at
www.whitecap.ca

The publisher acknowledges the support of the Canada Council for the
Arts and the Cultural Services Branch of the Government of British Columbia
for our publishing program. We acknowledge the financial support of the
Government of Canada through the Book Industry Development Program
for our publishing activities.

The author gratefully acknowledges the support of the British Columbia
Arts Council.

Contents

World of Difference

THERE'S NO DOUBT ABOUT IT: MOOSE ARE MASSIVE. They're the giants in a family that includes elk, caribou, and deer. A male moose, called a bull, can weigh up to 800 kilograms (1760 pounds). He can grow so tall his shoulder stands higher than a doorway. Antlers on the top of his head make him seem even taller.

Although a moose is huge, it looks funny—not frightful. It has long thin legs, a tiny tail, big ears, an outsized snout, and a furry flap that dangles from its throat. But a moose wears a lovely coat that comes in several shades of brown. Some coats are so

Moose are the world's biggest deer. The males grow enormous antlers, which adds to their height.

Most moose are loners, keeping to themselves for much of the year.

dark, they're almost black; others are so light, they're nearly white.

In winter, a thick, two-layered coat helps keep a moose cozy. Long, hollow hair blocks out cold winds, and short hair—like underwear—holds body heat in. When spring comes, the moose sheds its winter fur. A shorter, lighter coat is more comfortable in warm weather.

Moose don't spend much time in groups. In the fall mating season, a few gather together. Sometimes—mostly in winter—moose meet at the same feeding spots. But when they do, they are so busy munching they don't pay much attention to one another.

Through most of the year, female moose, called cows, live only with their calves. When newborns arrive in the spring, the older siblings wander off on their own.

ANTLERS OR HORNS?

Moose and other members of the deer family are the only animals that have antlers—branching headgear made of bone. Mostly it's just the males of the deer family that have them. Each year, the antlers fall off, then grow back again—almost always a bit bigger.

Antlers are different from horns, found on animals such as goats. Horns are hollow cases that form around a core of bone. They grow on both males and females. Horns don't branch out the way antlers do, and animals never shed them.

3

Where in the World

WOODS AND WETLANDS MAKE GREAT HOMES FOR MOOSE. They spend much of their time feeding among the trees and in the water. On their long legs, moose have no trouble walking through forests, simply stepping over any fallen trees. They can also wade easily in water. The large split hoofs of a moose spread as they move, helping them walk across soggy soil.

Despite their long legs and special hoofs, moose don't usually travel very far. They wander around—mostly at night— eating as they go.

Moving through snow is not a problem for a long-legged moose.

5

Sometimes moose choose to walk where the walking is easy—right down the road.

When the weather turns cold, moose search for winter shelter and food. They often head for evergreen forests. Needle-covered branches keep snow from piling deeply on the ground.

There are fewer places where moose can live in winter. Sometimes they must travel—either north or south—to find good spots. Moose that live among mountains may only need to move uphill or down.

If snow has piled up at a feeding place, moose may pack it down with their hoofs. Then they can move around more easily to reach their food.

Moose are not as common as they once were. However, some have moved into regions where none ever lived before. In North America, they're found in Canada and the northern United States. They also live in Asia and Europe, where people call them "elk."

MOOSE ON THE LOOSE

Moose don't make good city animals. They raid vegetable gardens in towns. They walk—even lie—on roads and airport runways. That puts their lives, as well as human lives, in danger.

People in Anchorage, Alaska, have been working to keep moose safe. They built passes beneath a busy highway so moose could walk under it. At the airport, they set up barbed-wire fences to help keep moose off the runways.

World Full of Food

MOOSE SPEND MOST OF THEIR TIME MUNCHING. In summer, a moose can eat at least 23 kilograms (50 pounds) of food every day. Even in winter—when there's less food around—a moose might gobble up 18 kilograms (40 pounds) a day.

Twigs on shrubs and trees—and some bark—make up the winter menu for moose. When the twigs are frozen, moose use their powerful jaws to snap them off. If there are farms and ranches nearby, they might eat winter hay put out for horses and cows.

Summertime brings a bigger choice of food. A moose can feast on the leaves as

Bare willow twigs make a crunchy winter meal for a hungry moose.

9

well as the twigs. Rising up on its back legs, it can reach leaves that are nearly 4 metres (13 feet) above the ground. It also nibbles fresh ferns and other low-growing forest plants. And it wades into ponds and lakes for food such as pondweed and water lilies—one of its favorites. It may even dive to reach the food it wants.

Moose munch leafy salads—whenever they are available.

A moose also lunches on grass, but its long legs get in the way. It has to kneel on its front legs—rear end in the air—and graze by pressing its chin along the ground. Sometimes the moose uses its nose or hoofs to dig out grass and other plants.

Salt is an important part of dinner for moose. They get some of it from eating salt-rich water plants. They also lick up salt in soil and on roads where workers have sprinkled it to melt snow and ice.

CHEWING IT TWICE

When a moose is busy finding food, it doesn't bother to stop and chew it well. Instead, it stores the meal in the first part of its big, four-part stomach.

Hours later—when the moose is feeling safe and comfortable—it brings a wad of swallowed food back into its mouth. The moose chews that thoroughly, then swallows it again. This time, the food moves right on through the rest of the stomach.

11

World of Words

This bull moose is not showing off his teeth. His curling lip says he's eager to find a mate.

MOST OF THE YEAR, MOOSE HAVE LITTLE TO SAY. That's because many moose, especially bulls, spend so much of their lives alone. When they gather at mating times, however, moose have plenty to say. And the talk is usually LOUD.

About the middle of September, bulls and cows start to search for one another. At first, they may be a long distance apart. The bulls roar and bellow. Sometimes they bark and croak. They make so much noise that other moose can hear them across a lake 3 kilometres (2 miles) wide.

Bulls also post messages. They leave

Sniff. Sniff. A bull moose tries to catch the scent of a female.

their body smells on rocks, shrubs, and trees throughout the woods. They beat or rub the bushes and trees with their antlers. It's how bulls tell cows, "We're eager to mate." To other bulls, their messages say, "We're ready to fight for a mate."

Meanwhile, the cows travel around, bellowing to attract bulls. They call out often with long, trembling moans. Sometimes, they also make noises that sound like coughing. When a bull and a cow finally meet, the bull follows her for a few days, grunting low.

Female moose talk to their calves—mostly by grunting. That's a cow's way of soothing her young. A newborn calf soon learns to call its mother. At first, it grunts softly. Then it cries loudly—especially when it's hungry or scared. Moose calves can sound a lot like human babies when they cry.

MOOSE MARVELS

Moose often amaze people. Here are just some of the reasons why:

- Antlers help moose keep cool in summer by getting rid of extra body heat.
- The many small blood vessels in the nose of a moose warm the winter air it breathes.
- Moose can run at speeds up to 55 kilometres (34 miles) an hour.
- Moose can live for more than 20 years in the wild.

15

World of Antlers

BEFORE BULLS GO COURTING, THEY POLISH THEIR ANTLERS. But they're not trying to look handsome. Moose use antlers to keep other bulls away from their mates—and some of these antlers are huge. Big bulls can have antlers that measure 2 metres (6 1/2 feet) across and weigh more than 25 kilograms (55 pounds).

Antlers do all their growing between spring and late summer. At first, they're covered with soft skin and fine hair, called velvet. When the antlers stop growing, the velvet dries and starts to peel. The bull helps remove it, rubbing his antlers against

Nothing is wrong here. It's just time for the covering on these antlers to peel off.

17

Battling bull
moose risk locking
their antlers
together. Then
they couldn't eat.

trees and bushes. By early fall, the bone is polished hard, and the moose is ready to search for a mate.

If two bulls choose the same mate, they threaten each other. They often turn their heads side to side to show off their big antlers, then rub them against a bush. Pressing their ears down and back, they might charge each other—without striking. That's often enough to make one of the moose run away.

Now and then, both of them stay to fight it out. They CLANG their antlers together, sometimes sending broken bits flying into the air. Head to head, they push, shove, and grunt. After stopping to whip the bushes with their antlers, they clash again and again. In the end, one of them usually gives up. Battles rarely last long enough for either bull to get seriously hurt.

MOOSE FOR MICE AND MOSS

What moose leave behind helps some animals and plants live. Antlers, which drop off in late fall and winter, make good food for gnawing animals such as mice and squirrels.

Some kinds of forest mosses grow mostly on moose droppings, or dung. Their seedlike spores stick to the feet of flies that land on the mosses. When these flies feed on fresh moose dung, they carry the spores with them.

New World

MOOSE DON'T GIVE BIRTH JUST ANYWHERE. They hunt for safe places hidden by bushes and trees. They favor quiet spots near water where they can eat and drink close to their newborn calves.

Between late May and early June, a skinny calf or two is born to a cow moose. She might even have triplets. Each calf weighs no more than a medium-sized dog. Its fur coat is a light reddish color, but it gradually changes to brown.

Just after a calf is born, it struggles to stand and take its first steps. A few days later, it can walk well—even run. It can

A cow moose pauses in a pond until her young calf catches up.

follow its mother as she feeds. If she must travel farther than the calf can walk, she hides it carefully first.

Drinking its mother's warm milk, a young calf grows fast. When it adds leaves and tender twigs to its meals, it can gain half a kilogram (more than a pound) a day.

These twin moose, only six or seven weeks old, wait for their mother's return.

All the while, the mother moose protects her calf. Her sight is not very good, but her strong sense of smell helps warn her of danger. So does her hearing. A cow's big ears can pick up far-off sounds.

If a wolf or bear threatens her calf, the cow moose might try to move it to safety. Usually, she stays and faces the enemy. Snorting madly, she rises high on her back legs. That's often enough to make the attacker run away. If not, the moose strikes with her sharp front hoofs.

Just two weeks old, a male calf lay hidden among bushes near a pond. He watched as his mother grazed in the water. Then he raised his head and cried. The cow moose ran to her calf and fed him milk until he fell asleep.

After his nap, the calf was ready to play. He dashed in and out of the water. He charged his mother, butting her with the top of his head. She gently butted back, then calmed the calf by licking him with her warm tongue.

Small World

A CALF GETS LESSONS ON LIFE FROM ITS MOM. During its first year, the calf is never very far from her. It watches what she does each day and learns by copying her.

The calf discovers how to protect itself. It sees how it will one day be able to use its hoofs to attack animals such as wolves. It also learns how to escape biting insects by rolling in mud puddles. Sometimes the calf plunges into water with its mother to avoid swarms of flies.

When it's swimming, a calf follows the cow moose, but it often gets tired before she does. It takes a rest by placing one leg

As a moose calf grows bigger, it gradually becomes more independent.

25

Bobbing up from a cool dive in the lake, this moose is feeling fine.

on her neck or by laying its chin on her back. Then it starts paddling again.

By mid-fall, a calf doesn't need milk any more. It has learned which plants to eat. At the end of its first year, it can weigh up to 17 times more than it did at birth. A human baby might increase its weight by only three times in the first year.

A one-year-old moose usually leaves its mother just before she gives birth again. If it doesn't go, she might charge—even kick—the calf to make it move out on its own.

Living by itself, the calf keeps growing fast. But it may not reach full size for another three or four years. The males grow button-sized antlers at first. Gradually, they produce the huge headgear that makes moose famous. With luck, they'll have many seasons to show off their antlers.

CHAMPION SWIMMERS

Moose don't look like great swimmers—but they are. They start to swim when they're only a few days old. Adults can slip through water at speeds up to 8 kilometres (5 miles) an hour. They may travel for two hours at a time. When looking for a new place to feed, they might swim right across a large lake.

Moose also dive, mostly to get water plants. They close their nostrils tight, then plunge as deep as 5.5 metres (18 feet).

27

Index